YORK NOTES

AQA POETRY ANTHOLOGY: RELATIONSHIPS

NOTES BY MARY GREEN

Longman
is an imprint of

PEARSON

York Press

YORK PRESS
322 Old Brompton Road, London SW5 9JH

PEARSON EDUCATION LIMITED
Edinburgh Gate, Harlow,
Essex CM20 2JE, United Kingdom
Associated companies, branches and representatives throughout the world

First published 2010

10 9 8 7 6

ISBN 978–1–4082–4877–5

Illustrated by Wes Lowe

Phototypeset by Chat Noir Design, France
Printed in China
CTPSC/06

Quotations from: 'Harmonium' by Simon Armitage, copyright © Simon Armitage, reproduced by permission of David Godwin Associates; 'The Manhunt' by Simon Armitage from *The Not Dead* (Pomona, 2008) copyright © Simon Armitage, 2008. Reproduced by permission of Pomona Books and David Godwin Associates; 'Hour' and 'Quickdraw' from *Rapture* (Picador, 2005), copyright © Carol Ann Duffy 2005, reproduced by permission of Picador, an imprint of Pan Macmillan, London; 'In Paris with You' by James Fenton, reprinted by permission of United Agents on behalf of James Fenton; 'Brothers' by Andrew Forster from *Fear of Thunder* reproduced by permission of Flambard Press; 'Ghazal', by Mimi Khalvati, copyright © Mimi Khalvati 2006, reproduced by kind permission of the author; 'The Farmer's Bride' by Charlotte Mew, reproduced by permission of Carcanet Press Ltd; 'Praise Song for My Mother' by Grace Nichols Copyright © Grace Nichols 1984, reproduced by permission of Curtis Brown Group Ltd; 'Nettles' by Vernon Scannell reproduced by permission of the Estate of Vernon Scannell

CONTENTS

PART THREE
KEY CONTEXTS AND THEMES

PART FOUR
LANGUAGE AND STRUCTURE

PART FIVE
GRADE BOOSTER

PART ONE: Introduction

Study and revision advice

There are two main stages to your reading and work on *Relationships*. Firstly, the study of the poems as you read them. Secondly, your preparation or revision for exam or controlled assessment. These top tips will help you with both.

 READING AND STUDYING THE POEMS – DEVELOP INDEPENDENCE!

- Try to engage and respond **personally** to the ideas and stories – not just for your enjoyment, but also because it helps you develop your own, **independent ideas and thoughts** about the poems. This is something that examiners are very keen to see.

- **Talk** about the poems with friends and family; ask questions in class; put forward your own viewpoint – and, if time, read around the poems to find out about *Relationships*.

- Take time to **consider** and **reflect** about the **key elements** of the cluster; keep your own notes, mind-maps, diagrams, scribbled jottings about the poems and how you respond to them; follow the story of each poem as it progresses (what do you think might happen?); discuss the main themes and ideas that interested the poet (what do you think it is about? Love? Breakdown? Family ties?); pick out language that impresses you or makes an impact, and so on.

- Treat your studying **creatively**. When you write essays or give talks about the cluster make your responses creative. Think about using really clear ways of explaining yourself, use unusual but apt **quotations**, well-chosen **vocabulary**, and try powerful, persuasive ways of beginning or ending what you say or write.

 REVISION – DEVELOP ROUTINES AND PLANS!

- **Good revision** comes from **good planning**. Find out when your exam or controlled assessment is and then plan to look at key aspects of the cluster on different days or times during your revision period. You could use these Notes – see **How can these Notes help me?** – and add dates or times when you are going to cover a particular topic.

- Use **different ways** of **revising**. Sometimes talking about the poems and what you know/don't know with a friend or member of the family can help; other times, filling a sheet of A4 with all your ideas in different colour pens about a particular poem, for example 'Sister Maude', can make ideas come alive; other times, making short lists of quotations to learn, or numbering events in the poem

- **Practice plans** and **essays**. As you get nearer the 'day', start by looking at essay questions and writing short bulleted plans. Do several plans (you don't have to write the whole essay); then take those plans and add details to them (quotations, linked ideas). Finally, using the advice in **Part Five: Grade Booster**, write some practice essays and then check them out against the advice we have provided.

 **EXAMINER'S TIP**

Prepare for the exam/assessment! Whatever you need to bring, make sure you have it with you – books, if you're allowed, pens, pencils – and that you turn up on time!

Introducing *Relationships*

This cluster of poems is about different kinds of human relationships and the range of feelings experienced Relationships are depicted between lovers or in marriage and the family, and one poem, 'Born Yesterday', is a dedication to a friend's child.

Elizabeth Barrett Browning: 'Sonnet 43'

'How do I love thee? Let me count the ways!'

Love in its various guises runs through most of the poems, but true love is explored in Elizabeth Barrett Browning's 'Sonnet 43' and Shakespeare's 'Sonnet 116'. The former expresses the joy and pleasure of a love that lasts. In the latter a love that lasts is what true love means.

James Fenton: 'In Paris with You'

'Don't talk to me of love. I've had an earful.'

Several poems deal with the disintegration of relationships. Some are bitter and angry, like 'Sister Maude' or 'Quickdraw'. Some are sorrowful and poignant, like 'The Farmer's Bride'. Others are bitter-sweet and even sardonic, like 'In Paris with You'.

Mimi Khalvati: 'Ghazal'

'What shape should I take to marry your own, have you
– hawk to my shadow, moth to my flame –
pursue me?'

'Ghazal' by Mimi Khalvati is haunted by desire, and desire is a common theme that runs through the poems. Sometimes it remains unsatisfied, as it is in 'Ghazal', or is fully realised, as in 'Hour'. At other times the reader is presented with potential lovers ever ready to grasp their chance, as the speakers are in 'To His Coy Mistress' and 'In Paris With You'.

Introducing the poets

Simon Armitage (b. 1963): 'Laura's poem: The Manhunt"

Simon Armitage, poet, novelist and playwright, was born in Huddersfield. His poetry often draws on everyday language to explore attitudes and feelings.

Elizabeth Barrett Browning (1806–61): 'Sonnet 43'

Elizabeth Barrett Browning was born in County Durham and married the poet Robert Browning. She was concerned with social issues, such as child labour, slavery and the position of women.

Carol Ann Duffy (b. 1955): 'Quickdraw' and 'Hour'

Carol Ann Duffy was born in Glasgow and brought up in Stafford. Much of her poetry is concerned with female experience. She was appointed poet laureate in 2009.

James Fenton (b. 1949): 'In Paris with You'

James Fenton, poet, critic and journalist, was born in London and brought up in Yorkshire. His interest in other cultures is reflected in his poetry.

Andrew Forster (b. 1964): 'Brothers'

Andrew Forster was brought up in Yorkshire and now lives in Scotland. He is interested in biographical poetry. His volume *Fear of Thunder* was shortlisted for the Forward Prize in 2008.

Mimi Khalvati (b. 1944): 'Ghazal'

Mimi Khalvati was born in Tehran, Iran, and brought up in Britain. She has worked in theatre and education. Her poetry is influenced by Persian literature and appeals strongly to the senses.

Philip Larkin (1922–85): 'Born Yesterday'

Philip Larkin was born in Coventry. He is regarded as one of the most important twentieth-century poets. His poetry often explores themes of unhappiness and discontent.

Andrew Marvell (1621–78): 'To His Coy Mistress'

Andrew Marvell was born in East Riding, Yorkshire. He wrote prose as well as poetry. His work is clever and witty and is often a commentary on the times he was living in.

Charlotte Mew (1869–1928): 'The Farmer's Bride'

Charlotte Mew was born in Bloomsbury, London. She was not well known during her lifetime, although her work was admired by many poets. However, she received greater critical attention in the twentieth century.

Grace Nichols (b. 1950): 'Praise Song for My Mother'

Grace Nichols was born in Guyana and lives in the UK. Much of her work reflects Caribbean life and customs. She has a strong interest in tales and myths.

Christina Rossetti (1830–94): 'Sister Maude'

Christina Rossetti was born in London. Religious themes are often present in her poems. She was also interested in social issues (such as child labour) and did voluntary work.

Vernon Scannell (1922–2007): 'Nettles'

Vernon Scannell was born in Lincolnshire. As a young man he was a professional boxer and he wrote sporting novels as well as poetry.

William Shakespeare (1564–1616): 'Sonnet 116'

William Shakespeare was born in Stratford-upon-Avon and is regarded as the greatest English writer. He is admired for the richness of his language and the breadth and depth of his ideas.

PART TWO: THE POEMS

Grace Nichols: 'Praise Song for My Mother'

SUMMARY

1. The poem is a daughter's tribute to her mother.

2. The first four verses recall the mother's special qualities.

3. The final line recalls the mother's advice.

WHAT IS SPECIAL ABOUT THIS POEM?

A The poem is a tender **praise song**, a traditional African poem created in **celebration** of someone or something.

B It discusses the **theme** of **mother-love.**

C The **voice** is strong and celebratory.

D The poem refers to **nature** to create **metaphors**, which reveal the mother's qualities.

E It is **structured** as three verses of three lines, followed by a verse of four lines, and a single line at the end.

KEY QUOTE

'You were
the fishes red gill
   to me
the flames tree's
   spread to me
the crab's leg/
   the fried
   plantain smell
replenishing
   replenishing'

METAPHORS FROM NATURE

Metaphor is a powerful literary technique and it makes the mother's qualities especially vivid. This suits the praise song, since it needs to capture the essence of a person.

The metaphors are drawn from the natural world, allowing the poet to create images that are elemental, i.e. to do with the elements, as nature is. In the opening verse the mother is depicted as water, 'deep and bold and fathoming', revealing a woman with insight and courage. Some images such as 'the flame tree's spread' suggest a Caribbean setting.

Each metaphor identifies a particular quality. By the fourth verse several metaphors follow in quick succession. One, 'the fishes red gill', for example, evokes the image of the mother as the breath of life, for gills are the means by which fish breathe.

THE POEM'S MOVEMENT

The first three verses have a repeating form. Apart from the capital letter at the beginning of each verse, there is no punctuation and therefore no pauses. This creates a steady, rhythmic movement.

As the poem gathers momentum in the fourth verse, 'to me' is dropped in the fourth line and replaced with a forward slash. The effect is to create a close connection between different foods and their smell, helping to suggest images of maternal nourishment.

The last line is set apart and the mother's words are spoken. There is a pause. The poem slows, and closes.

EXAMINER'S TIP: WRITING ABOUT THE VOICE OF THE POEM

It can be difficult to write about the 'voice' of the poem. You need to concentrate to hear it. Read the poem aloud and think about what feeling is being projected. Is it sad, thoughtful, witty? Is there a change in tone?

Here the female voice is strong and clear from the outset. But it is also intimate and personal, so that the reader cannot help but identify it as the voice of the poet as well as the daughter. Addressing the mother, 'You were … to me', at the beginning of the first three verses shows deep affection for the mother's 'replenishing' or care. It is written in the past tense, evoking a sense of looking back. Perhaps the mother has died.

In the last line we hear the mother's voice through the speaker. An imperative is used, which sounds a note of fearlessness. The voice is also like a blessing that sends the daughter out into the world to experience the richness of life.

CHECKPOINT 1

What motherly quality does 'the flame tree's spread' evoke?

? DID YOU KNOW?

The forward slash was used in the Middle Ages to denote a comma. Today it is used in several ways, sometimes to show a strong connection between words or phrases.

COMPARE THIS POEM WITH . . .

Nettles – about a father protecting his son.
Born Yesterday – written in dedication to a newborn child.

GLOSSARY

flame tree a tree with flame-coloured blossoms and a wide canopy, found in the Caribbean

Philip Larkin: 'Born Yesterday'

SUMMARY

1. The speaker makes a wish for a newborn baby, Sally Amis.

2. The first verse describes the usual wishes people make when a new baby is born.

3. The second verse tells us the wish the speaker has chosen – that the baby will grow up to be ordinary.

4. The reason for the choice is explored.

WHAT IS SPECIAL ABOUT THIS POEM?

A The poem is a **dedication** and its **theme** is finding happiness through being ordinary.

B It is written in **two verses**; the first has ten lines. The second verse is expressed as a **sonnet** in fourteen lines with a **rhyming couplet** at the end.

C The poem's **rhythm** reaches its height near the **end**.

D The poem has powerful **adjectives** and uses techniques to create compelling sound effects.

E The **voice** is **colloquial** but also **thoughtful**, and **addresses** the **baby**.

OPPOSITES

In 'Born Yesterday', the theme centres around the wish for the newborn child: finding happiness. But how might this be achieved? Happiness is intangible and difficult to define, and the speaker's suggestion comes as something of a surprise: by being ordinary.

To be ordinary in the usual sense is to be commonplace and unexciting, not something most people aspire to and certainly not something we associate with happiness. In the second verse this **paradox** is explored.

Happiness is not necessarily available to those who are talented or beautiful. If you are ordinary, you have nothing special about you to distort your view of yourself or your expectations; nothing to stop you getting on with life. The poem is summed up as the speaker suggests that by being ordinary, you might achieve the extraordinary something special and elusive.

TAKING FLIGHT

The poem opens with an even, leisurely rhythm, as if the speaker might be chatting to the baby in her cot. There are several pauses in the first verse that accentuate this and also help to emphasise **colloquial** expressions such as in line 10.

Through most of the second verse this rhythm is maintained, although the voice becomes more thoughtful. However, the last four lines provide a dramatic shift in tempo.

EXAMINER'S TIP

Commit poems or key quotes to memory. They may not be available in the exam.

A pause occurs with the use of the dash in the preceding line and the poem begins to fly as a series of positive adjectives in lines 21–3 seem to take off. It is as though happiness has been caught in mid-air. In the last line the poem descends, landing with the final two words, and the reader is left feeling that they have read something profound. Try reading the poem yourself in this way.

EXAMINER'S TIP: WRITING ABOUT SOUND EFFECTS

Sometimes you can study the same lines from different points of view. For example, the last four lines, as well as having a compelling rhythm, have compelling sounds. The series of adjectives, which mean in turn adept, alert, adaptable and low-key, are associated with the idea of being 'dull'. However, the sound of the adjectives suggests much more exciting qualities.

This is due partly to the adjectives being polysyllabic. They are a pleasure to say, and tumble out one after the other. But it is also due to the repetition in the use of the letter 'l' and to a lesser extent the letter 's'. The effect is a lush, exhilarating sound.

The final adjective in line 23, whose meaning is 'spellbound', serves to confirm this exhilaration. It is an example of consonance with 'dull' and 'skilled', and it rhymes with 'called', which provides the closing sound. The overall effect is that these musical adjectives suggest being 'dull' is more satisfying than we might think and may be the route to happiness.

KEY CONNECTIONS

Would you want your child, boy or girl, to be ordinary? Read Helen Rumbelow's article 'Do I want you to be an A-star baby?' in which she questions Philip Larkin's wish for Sally Amis. Search for it on the Times Online website.

CHECKPOINT 2

What does the image 'Tightly-folded bud' conjure up? Why is a 'bud' (rather than a flower, for example) especially appropriate?

COMPARE THIS POEM WITH . . .

Praise Song for My Mother – a daughter's tribute to her mother.

Nettles – about a father protecting his son.

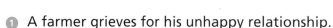

Charlotte Mew: 'The Farmer's Bride'

SUMMARY

1. A farmer grieves for his unhappy relationship.

2. He has married a young woman three years earlier.

3. But she is afraid of intimacy and runs away, until a search party finds her and brings her home.

4. She is happy to make friends with birds and animals but fears men.

5. While his wife sleeps, the farmer is filled with longing.

WHAT IS SPECIAL ABOUT THIS POEM?

A The poem is a **narrative poem** and a **lament** written in six rhyming verses.

B The **voice** of the poem is the **farmer's**, speaking in **dialect**.

C The **theme** is **unfulfilled love**.

D The **setting** is **rural** and the **seasons** echo the theme of the poem.

E The poem has many moving **images** from **nature**.

A RURAL VOICE

The farmer's character is brought to life through his voice and dialect, which is often combined with rich **imagery**. For example, the line beginning 'When us was wed …' is **juxtaposed** with the powerful imagery of his young wife's rejection, 'Of love and me and all things human'. This technique gives the voice a simple eloquence.

GRADE BOOSTER

To support your ideas, find several more images that depict the wife and record them. Are they always of animals?

KEY QUOTE

''Tis but a stair
Betwixt us … the
    down,
The soft young
    down of her;
    the brown,
The brown of her
    – her eyes, her
    hair, her hair!'

The events unfold through the farmer's perspective, and in the second verse the voices of the local search party are reported as well. In marked contrast, the wife remains dumb like the animals that she feels close to.

Towards the end of the poem the voice becomes agitated with longing. The farmer watches his wife asleep, moved by and drawn to 'The soft young down of her'. As the final verse gathers pace and his passion increases, the lines sound a disturbing note. What might he do?

SETTING AND SEASON

The rural setting is the backdrop of the poem, which opens as harvest is underway. When autumn is referred to again, it is a grimmer time of 'short days' and 'low grey sky', followed by frost on winter's 'black earth'.

Against this earth lie a 'magpie's spotted feathers'. So the scene is black and white – monochrome – reflecting the farmer's sorrow and loveless marriage. The only colour is in the red berries, a metaphor for sexual experience and reproduction. They ripen at Christmas, also a time of new birth, but there is no offspring for the farmer and his wife. Like the 'black earth', they remain barren.

Spring is mentioned earlier in the poem, in reference to the wife's youthfulness, 'Sweet as the first wild violets'. But this is not for the husband's delight. She takes no pleasure in his company.

EXAMINER'S TIP: WRITING ABOUT THE WIFE'S CHARACTER

When writing about the young wife, make sure that you refer to the images used to depict her, drawing out what they have common.

Similes are often used. She is like 'a little frightened fay', and later 'Shy as a leveret'. Animal similes build up to create a motif of the wife as a small wild creature, trembling, 'All in a shiver and a scare', distressed and untameable.

It is not only the husband that the wife fears. As long as 'men-folk keep away', she is happy, which suggests an earlier story, of cruelty or abuse, perhaps. What we do know is that she is 'Too young maybe' for marriage and that life has damaged her.

KEY QUOTE

'The berries redden up to Christmas-time. What's Christmas-time without there be Some other in the house than we!'

CHECKPOINT 3

What other images of winter are there? How do they link to the meaning of the poem?

EXAMINER'S TIP

Remember, if several images relate to the same idea in a poem, then they are part of a motif.

COMPARE THIS POEM WITH . . .

Hour – about the intensity of new love.
Sonnet 43 – about the quality of true love.

GLOSSARY

fay a fairy
rime a grey-white frost

James Fenton: 'In Paris with You'

SUMMARY

① The speaker is in Paris with a new love.

② He has been hurt by a previous lover and cannot talk of love.

③ He does not wish to visit tourist sights and would rather stay in the hotel room so they can find out about each other.

④ His passionate feelings increase as he sweet-talks his new love.

WHAT IS SPECIAL ABOUT THIS POEM?

A The poem's **theme** is love on the **rebound**.
B It has an **insistent rhythm** helped along by **rhyme**.
C The **voice** is **colloquial** and **humorous**.

ON THE REBOUND

While the words tell us that the speaker is 'wounded', 'bamboozled' and 'on the rebound', the comic movement of the poem gives the theme a light treatment. So initially it seems to the reader **ironic** that the speaker should talk of lost love in such a lively way.

However, this conflict between the two features suggests we can read the poem in various ways. Is the speaker truly on the rebound? Is a painful experience hidden under the light tone? What does the speaker want from the new love?

JOGGING ALONG

The poem jogs along because the metre is very regular and insistent. The first two lines are **iambic penatameter**. These are followed by two much shorter lines that are not only bouncy, but rise at the end as though the speaker was overstating his point.

The jogging movement is also helped by frequent use of rhyme, some of it comic, where the rhyme is contrived to fit, such as 'wounded'/'maroonded'. The whole effect is to create a light, sardonic tone to the theme.

EXAMINER'S TIP: WRITING ABOUT THE VOICE

The voice is casual and the language everyday, but you should also note its **tone**. It is peevish and self-pitying, as the new love hears how they cannot 'talk of love' because the speaker has been badly hurt. But since the first verse ends on a hopeful note that is repeated throughout the poem, we might wonder how deep the wound is.

In the third verse there is a grouchy edge to the voice, irritated by the thought of visits to the Parisian tourist sights. On the other hand a 'sleazy' hotel room might offer intimate pleasures, and by the end of the poem the speaker, while still claiming he doesn't wish 'to talk of love', does exactly that.

CHECKPOINT 4

What do you think the line 'are *we* bound' (a reversal of 'we're bound') means?

COMPARE THIS POEM WITH . . .

To His Coy Mistress – life is short, so pursue your desires.
Hour – about the intensity of new love.

GLOSSARY

on the rebound getting together with someone simply to replace a more important relationship that has just ended

Vernon Scannell: 'Nettles'

SUMMARY

- The speaker tells us how his son has fallen in the nettle bed.
- The boy seeks comfort from his parents.
- The speaker sharpens his scythe and cuts down the nettles.
- He piles them up and burns them.
- In two weeks new nettles have grown again.

WHAT IS SPECIAL ABOUT THIS POEM?

A The **theme** is **parental love** and **protection**.
B The poem is told through the **father's eyes**.
C Powerful **literary techniques** such as **metaphor**, **motif** and **personification** are used to describe the nettles.
D It is written in four **quatrains** of **iambic pentameter**.

THE FATHER'S VOICE

The father recounts the events of the incident and his voice is both loving and angry: loving, when the speaker sees the blisters on the child's 'tender skin', and full of 'fury' as the nettles are hacked down.

The same voice also makes the important observation in the last line about the difficulties that life will bring. This together with the motif of war leaves the reader wondering what the speaker's experience has been.

METAPHOR AND MOTIF

Although the events tell us a story about a child falling in a bed of nettles, the images in the poem suggest a much deeper meaning. All the most powerful images are **metaphors** associated with war. The nettles are a 'regiment of spite' and a 'fierce parade', intended to hurt. When they are cut down they are 'the fallen dead', the casualties of war.

This **personification** of nettles as soldiers also gives the images greater impact, and the regular repetition of war images builds to create a **motif**. The 'sharp wounds' in the final line, therefore, signify not only the pain the nettles cause, but also the harsh realities the child will meet in life.

EXAMINER'S TIP: WRITING ABOUT THE THEME

Where there is a **motif**, remember that it will be connected to the poem's **theme**. For example, we could say that the theme of the poem is parental love.

However, the motif of war in the poem tells a bigger story. Here parental love is about the need to protect the child against life's difficulties, something no parent can do. This is symbolised by the nettles and their capacity to re-grow.

Carol Ann Duffy: 'Hour'

SUMMARY

1. Two lovers spend an hour together in the open air.
2. The hour is rich with sensuality.

WHAT IS SPECIAL ABOUT THIS POEM?

A The poem is a **love poem** written as a **sonnet**.
B The **themes** are being **in love** and how **time** is distorted.
C The **voice** is **passionate**, spoken by one lover to another in the **present tense**.
D Several **literary techniques** are used to create **memorable** images.

BEING IN LOVE

The theme of the poem is the intensity of being in love and its relationship with time. When two lovers are together the present seems to stretch, so that time is distorted. An hour is perceived as 'thousands of seconds' and time seems magical. It is reminiscent of fairy-tale or mythic time in which the lover's hair is 'like treasure' and the light is a 'Midas' light.

But time and love are linked in more than one way. An underlying theme in the poem is that love cannot last, for time is the enemy of love, 'hates' it, wants it made 'poor'. This is also hinted at when the lovers bribe the night to stay away, so that 'nothing dark' can end their intensity.

For the present, however, while passion lasts, love will defy time.

KEY QUOTE

'For thousands of seconds we kiss; your hair like treasure on the ground'

GRADE BOOSTER

Make links! Find quotations from different poems that describe the same ideas, such as 'love'. Note their similarities or differences in two columns.

KEY CONNECTIONS

In the Brothers Grimm fairy tale *Rumpelstiltskin*, the miller's daughter is told to spin gold from straw.

A MODERN SONNET

Why has the poet chosen the sonnet form? Traditionally, many love poems are written as sonnets. This poem is close to the traditional Shakespearean sonnet form with a rhyme scheme *abab cdcd efef gg*, although the rhymes *a, c* and *e* are half-rhymes here.

Since a sonnet also explores a particular idea, we need to see how this happens in 'Hour'. The first two quatrains set down the point of view or thought: being in love has such a powerful effect that time shifts, seems to slow down.

The third quatrain begins 'so' (meaning therefore or consequently) and says that nothing can diminish the power of the present, despite the dark that threatens.

The thought is carried over into the final couplet in a **run-on line**, where the 'here' and 'Now' – the continuous moment in which the lovers seem to exist – is reinforced.

EXAMINER'S TIP: WRITING ABOUT IMAGERY AND TECHNIQUE

You should try to say how the images relate to the meaning of the poem and identify some of the poetic techniques used. Since the poem is a love poem, in which the nature of love, and the loved one, is described, we might expect the imagery to be rich.

Appropriately, richness itself provides the **motif** running through the poem and this applies to the theme of time as well as that of love. In the first verse, the hour the lovers spend together is so powerful that it is 'bright as a dropped coin', and this **simile** 'makes love rich'.

Other techniques are also used. The 'Midas light' is a **metaphor** for the sun that turns 'limbs to gold', and the 'cuckoo spit' is a pearl earring, while **alliteration** – 'light', 'limbs', 'candle', 'cuckoo' – heightens the pleasure of the 'shining hour'. In the final line the **repetition** of 'gold' expresses the joy in love's power to transform us; to spin 'gold from straw'.

KEY QUOTE

'no jewel hold a candle to the cuckoo spit hung from the blade of grass at your ear'

CHECKPOINT 5

The first person plural, 'we', is used several times in the poem. Why do you think this is?

COMPARE THIS POEM WITH . . .

Sonnet 116 – the idea that love doesn't alter.
To His Coy Mistress – life is short so fulfil your desire while you can.

GLOSSARY

Midas the story of King Midas is a Greek myth. When his wish that everything he touches turns to gold is granted, he dies, since food and drink also become gold

William Shakespeare: 'Sonnet 116'

SUMMARY

1. The speaker says that he does not wish to present obstacles to marriage for those who truly love.

2. He says that love does not alter even if things around it change.

3. It remains steadfast against difficulties.

4. Love does not diminish with the passing of time and fading beauty.

5. If this is not true, then the speaker denies that he has ever written, and that there is any such thing as love.

WHAT IS SPECIAL ABOUT THIS POEM?

A The poem's theme is the **nature** of **true love**.
B It contrast love's **faithfulness** with ideas about **change**.
C It is written in traditional sonnet form, in iambic pentameter.
D The voice is **forceful** and spoken in the **present tense**; it seems to speak **directly** to the reader.
E It uses several **literary techniques** such as personification and allusion.
F The poem has a witty ending.

NO ROOM FOR DOUBT?

From the first line, the voice is strong and soon states what love is not: it does not waver. The steady iambic pentameter reinforces this voice as we are taken through series of images that also exemplify love's steadfastness.

? DID YOU KNOW ?

'Sonnet 116' is one of the 152 sonnets written by Shakespeare (usually called *The Sonnets*). Most are concerned with some aspect of love or beauty, and also the passing of time. The dedication at the front of the sonnets, 'To Mr W.H.', is surrounded by controversy. Who this was remains a mystery.

The exclamation 'O no' in the fifth line sounds a protest. Love is 'never shaken', assures the speaker, forestalling any objections to what is being said. The rhyming couplet at the end goes further and plays a clever trick. If the speaker's words are untrue, then the poet has never written and no one has ever truly loved. But since he has written, then the speaker must be right.

However, maybe there are other ways of considering the voice, particularly at the end. If true love is such perfection, how can it exist? Is there a hint of disappointment, expressed in the final couplet that ideal love (and writing) is impossible to achieve? Read the poem again and see what you think.

CREATING EFFECTS

Several literary techniques are used to create effects of different sorts in the poem. The opening line runs into the next then stops. This **caesura** gives weight to the words that follow, 'love is not love'. They in turn run into the next line, to emphasise love's constancy.

Perhaps the most important way in which Love is given status, however, is through **personification**. It is personified with Time, but is greater than Time, able to resist its destructive power, 'even to the edge of doom'.

This reference to death occurs again in the **allusion** to the Grim Reaper, traditionally depicted as a macabre, cloaked skeleton carrying a sickle or scythe. Although youth and beauty are destroyed by Time, Love is not.

EXAMINER'S TIP: WRITING ABOUT THEMES

Make sure you have identified not only the main theme, but also any other themes associated with it.

For example, the poem attempts to define what true love is. In so doing the speaker claims that it does not change, even if the world around it does. So there is a contrast between the theme of love's steadfastness and the theme of change.

A contrast exists, for example, between love that is 'ever-fixed', and the instability of 'tempests', or between the (pole) star's steady guide and a 'wand'ring' ship. Similar contrasts are repeated throughout the poem. They all serve to define love.

CHECKPOINT 6

What does the image 'brief hours and weeks' refer to? How is 'Love' affected by it?

★ **GRADE BOOSTER**

Poems have layers of meaning. Consider a poem from more than one point of view before you decide what it is saying.

COMPARE THIS POEM WITH . . .

Hour – about the intensity of new love.
Quickdraw – about the disintegration of love.

GLOSSARY

remove shift direction (when change or 'alteration' is found)
mark beacon, light or signal
bark ship
sickle (scythe) a long-handled tool with a curved blade used for cutting grass or crops

Simon Armitage: 'Laura's poem: The Manhunt'

SUMMARY

1. The poem is about the intimate relationship between the speaker, Laura, and her lover.

2. It describes the physical war wounds the lover has suffered in the upper part of his body.

3. Finally it describes the mental wound the lover has suffered, and its effect.

WHAT IS SPECIAL ABOUT THIS POEM?

A The poem's forceful **theme** is the **renewing** of a relationship after the **effects** of war.

B It is a **free verse** poem that contains rhyme.

C Its vivid **imagery** is related the human body, to the mechanics of familiar objects and to **war**.

D The poem also contains **ambiguity** that draws us in.

E The poem is told with great **feeling** and **sensitivity** by Laura.

WAR WOUNDS

The title contains the first powerful image. It tells us not only that it is told through a woman's eyes, the wife or lover of the soldier depicted, but also that she is searching for the man she knew. There are other **connotations** in the word 'Manhunt'. A manhunt is the stalking of a wanted man. War is also predatory. Its business is to seek out the enemy.

KEY QUOTE

'and handle and hold
the damaged porcelain collar-bone,
and mind and attend
the fractured rudder of shoulder-blade'

KEY CONNECTIONS

Search The Times Online website for an interesting article, 'Battlefield Salvos', written by Simon Armitage, on the background to this poem and the film *Forgotten Heroes: The Not Dead* associated with it.

mages of the wounded lover revolve around his broken body and the workings of
amiliar objects: the 'blown hinge' of the jaw, the 'fractured rudder of shoulder-
lade'. They also remind us of the fragility of the human body in which the collar-
one is fine china and the lungs 'parachute silk'.

The bullet is a 'foetus' – something that grows – and therefore has sinister
mplications. It links to the 'sweating, unexploded mine / buried deep', something
hat could blast at any moment. And 'every nerve' has tightened around the trauma,
vhich cannot be expressed. These images imply pent-up violence and anger and an
nability to speak of the experience.

MYSTERY AND AMBIGUITY

he soldier-lover remains both silent and unknown. While the reader traces his
nasculine physicality through 'Laura's' voice, he is passive. We do not know what his
esponses are, only his wounds, and his unspoken words tell us that these wounds
un deep. His silence also allows the reader to 'come close' to the gravity and
estruction of war, in a way that his words might not.

he words 'come close' end the poem. But for the reader, the poem is not finished.
Ve want to know what it is Laura comes close to. Is it love? Pity? Understanding?
ntimacy with her lover? This mystery or ambiguity remains, however many times
ve read the poem, because there is no answer. We cannot know what he feels and
here is no way of fully articulating the suffering of war.

EXAMINER'S TIP: WRITING ABOUT THE STRUCTURE OF THE POEM

Although this is a free verse poem, with irregular rhythm and lines of different
length, it does contain patterns that create particular effects.

The rhythms of some lines are repeated, for example the pairs between lines
seven and twelve. This, along with the repetition of 'and' and 'the' at the
beginning of these lines gives the poem intensity. It also makes the lines
memorable. As do the rhymes. Some are full rhymes – 'trace'/'face',
'lung'/'thumb'. Some are half-rhymes – 'hurt'/'heart'.

All these patterns combine to give structure to the poem and help to move it
along smoothly. They also give eloquence to a poem dealing with a very painful
subject. Search for other patterns in the poem.

CHECKPOINT 7

Which other poem in the cluster has images of war?

 DID YOU KNOW?

Some of the greatest English poetry has been written by war poets: Ivor Gurney, Wilfred Owen, Isaac Rosenberg, Siegfried Sassoon, Edward Thomas, Alun Lewis, Keith Douglas. For poets of the First World War, see *Men Who March Away* (1965) edited by I. M. Parsons.

 **GRADE BOOSTER**

Remember that sometimes **ambiguity** is part of the poem because there are no definitive answers.

COMPARE THIS POEM WITH . . .

Nettles – about a father protecting his son.
Sonnet 116 – the idea that love doesn't alter.

Christina Rossetti: 'Sister Maude'

SUMMARY

1. The speaker's secret love has been revealed to her parents by her sister Maude.

2. The lover has died.

3. The speaker scolds her sister and says that her lover did not desire Maude anyway.

4. She says that Maude will suffer sleepless nights.

5. She declares that sister Maude will be denied entry to Heaven.

KEY QUOTE

'If my dear and I knocked at Heaven-gate Perhaps they'd let us in: But sister Maude, oh sister Maude, Bide *you* with death and sin.'

EXAMINER'S TIP

Reread your work as you write. Does it make sense? Have you said what you mean? Have you referred to examples from the poem?

WHAT IS SPECIAL ABOUT THIS POEM?

A The poem is written as a short ballad.
B Its theme is a **sister's betrayal**.
C The background and details of the story are **mysterious** and **ambiguous**.
D It includes potent **religious** imagery.
E The voice is **angry** and **emotional**.

UNANSWERED QUESTIONS

The reader's interest is aroused from a first reading of the poem. The speaker's hatred of her sister and the gulf that has developed between them is clear. But the background and details are not. Who are Maude and her sister? Who is the lover? Why has he died? Is it at Maude's hand? In the third verse jealousy is implied, but beyond the lover's lack of interest in Maude, no more is said.

Not only has the lover died, but also the father is in 'Paradise', and the mother is at 'Heaven-gate'. Is this a result of Maude's betrayal? Have they died of shame? This withholding of information is effective. It creates continual ambiguity, lends mystery to the poem and increases its power.

RELIGIOUS IMAGERY

Using religious imagery also increases the poem's mystery. The simile of the dead lover, 'as cold as stone' with his 'clotted curls', is reminiscent of the life-size stone effigies found on medieval tombs. The discussion of the soul suggests that the crime committed, whatever they are, will have repercussions beyond the grave. 'Paradise' and 'Heaven-gate' are contrasted with the speaker's wish that Maude ends up in hell.

EXAMINER'S TIP: WRITING ABOUT THE VOICE

Think about the speaker's voice in 'Sister Maude', looking for evidence beyond the obvious. It is not only emotional and angry. It is vengeful. Looking for complex meanings will impress the examiner.

GRADE BOOSTER

Poetry rarely has clear meanings. You can ask different or even opposing questions in your writing and explore them when studying a poem. To help you, use phrases such as: 'the words suggest', 'we might infer' or 'the lines imply'.

Elizabeth Barrett Browning: 'Sonnet 43'

SUMMARY

1. The speaker lists the different attributes of her love.
2. These cover a range of feelings and situations.
3. The love will become even greater after death.

WHAT IS SPECIAL ABOUT THIS POEM?

A Its theme is the **nature** of **true love**.
B It is a Petrarchan sonnet written in two quatrains and a sestet.
C It uses vivid **religious** imagery.
D The voice is **intense** but also **reflective**.

THE NATURE OF LOVE

The poem explores the nature of love and the different ways the speaker experiences it. Initially, the degree of love is gauged through the 'depth', 'breadth' and 'height' the 'soul can reach', so it is beyond the physical.

Sometimes it is a quiet love that exists in the everyday experience with the loved one, or it touches the speaker as a link to the past and innocent childhood belief. At the end it is a love that the speaker hopes will be even greater 'after death'.

RELIGION AND IMAGERY

The religious imagery helps to convey the profound love the speaker feels. Reference to the 'soul' immediately gives the love a spiritual dimension. The third and fourth lines suggest a soul that is beyond understanding or 'out of sight' in the context of, for example, the perfect state of Christian 'Grace' or salvation. There are also double meanings in the poem. While we associate 'passion' with the intensity of human love it also refers to Christ's Passion, his suffering up to the crucifixion. 'Passion' therefore links to the idea of suffering and the speaker's 'old griefs' or sorrows. So perhaps the love felt is also a consoling love.

EXAMINER'S TIP: WRITING ABOUT THE STRUCTURE OF THE POEM

You should mention that the poem is a Petrarchan sonnet that follows a pattern. Here the theme – the nature of love – is set out in the first quatrain and an exploration of its nature begun. The exploration is developed in the second quatrain, where love is viewed from different perspectives. The sestet begins in the ninth line and shifts slightly in mood. The love felt is seen as a reminder of past emotions and faith, and the sonnet culminates in a declaration of intense love beyond the grave.

KEY QUOTE

'– and, if God choose,
I shall but love thee better after death.'

KEY CONNECTIONS

'Sonnet 43' is found in Elizabeth Barrett Browning's *Sonnets from the Portuguese*, published in 1850, and is included in *The Nation's Favourite Poems*, published in 1995.

COMPARE THIS POEM WITH . . .

Sister Maude – about a sister's betrayal.
In Paris with You – about love on the rebound.

GLOSSARY

the ends of Being death
Grace in the Christian religion the love, favour and mercy of God in eternal life

Carol Ann Duffy: 'Quickdraw'

SUMMARY

1. The speaker keeps two phones to hand waiting for the lover to ring.

2. When the lover rings the voice is angry and hurtful.

3. The speaker puts on the answer phone but answers the next call anyway and the lover retaliates, wounding the speaker.

4. The speaker has another concealed mobile but the lover texts both phones, delivering the final attack.

WHAT IS SPECIAL ABOUT THIS POEM?

A The poem's **theme** is the **disintegration** of a damaged relationship.
B The striking **imagery** and events are drawn from a **typical Western**.
C The **structure** of the poem **mirrors** the theme.
D The **voice** is alert and agitated, as if the speaker is **facing danger**.

BREAKING DOWN

The main theme of the poem, the disintegration of a relationship, is told by the speaker, who is one of the lovers. It is depicted as the finale of a Western, the shoot-out.

The theme also involves the hurt felt by the speaker. Kisses are 'bullets'. The lover's voice is 'a pellet', able to deliver cutting remarks that wound.

The reader continually feels that the lover has the upper hand in this relationship and the speaker is the greater victim. Every attempt the speaker makes to fight back is forestalled. At the end of the poem the speaker is down, as a dying gunfighter might be, broken by the relationship.

DEATH BY WORDS

The poem is highly visual. From the first verse the imagery conjures up two lovers in a vicious slanging match, their 'phones, / like guns'. Although the setting is a room somewhere, all the connotations are of a Western. Even the title reminds us of this. Love has become 'calamity', a disaster in the 'Last Chance saloon', where hope is all but lost. These linked images form an extended metaphor.

Powerful verbs are used. The 'twirl' of the phone is a gunslinger's action. The 'trigger' of the 'tongue' fires insults and the 'blast' 'through the heart' is also a verbal one. These lovers do not end the relationship amicably. Rather, they fight it out to the death with words.

EXAMINER'S TIP: WRITING ABOUT THE STRUCTURE OF THE POEM

It is particularly important to discuss the structure and movement of this poem, the effects created and how they link to the theme.

For example, the verses usually run erratically one into the other, as in: 'then blast me // through the heart'. Or there is an abrupt, unexpected pause, for example at the end of verse one, before the thought is carried into the next verse, to read: '… and hear me groan. // You've wounded me.' There are also frequent pauses and sudden halts within lines (provided by commas and full stops) as well as enjambment.

Consequently the rhythm is jerky, and the internal rhyme (such as 'noon'/ 'saloon', 'tone'/'phone') scattered throughout the poem gives emphasis.

All these techniques merge to create a disjointed, fast-shooting effect that mirrors the theme. As the poem progresses, so the relationship disintegrates and is played out in the gunfight. In the final verse the lover is the victor. The speaker 'reel[s]' and the lover fires the final volley: 'Take this … / and this … and this … and this … and this …'

CHECKPOINT 8

The poem could be called 'At the Last Chance Saloon'. Why might this be a suitable title? Think of more than one reason.

KEY QUOTE

'I reel.
Down on my knees, I fumble for the phone, read the silver bullets of your kiss. Take this …
and this … and this … and this … and this …'

COMPARE THIS POEM WITH . . .

Hour – about the intensity of new love.
Laura's poem: The Manhunt – about renewing a relationship after the effects of war.

Simon Armitage: 'Harmonium'

SUMMARY

1. An old harmonium is sold to the speaker for a small amount.

2. When the speaker collects it from the church he considers how it has aged.

3. But it can still be played, as it once was, accompanying the generations of fathers and sons who sang in the choir.

4. The speaker's own father helps to carry away the harmonium and muses on how the next box the son will carry will be the father's coffin.

5. The speaker reflects on the inadequacy of his reply to his father's comment.

WHAT IS SPECIAL ABOUT THIS POEM?

A The speaker is the son.
B The poem's poignant **theme** is the relationship between father and son.
C The harmonium is an important **motif** that links generations.
D The poem is **free verse** but includes patterns of rhythm, and also rhyme.
E Techniques such as **alliteration** and **assonance** create sound effects.

STRIKING A CHORD

We can think of the harmonium as a **metaphor** for the speaker's father. The harmonium keys are 'yellowed … finger nails'. The father has 'smoker's fingers'. The harmonium is carried flat on its back, as the old father will be in his coffin.

KEY QUOTE

'where father and son,
each in their time, had opened their throats
and gilded finches – like high notes – had streamed out.'

KEY QUOTE

'And I, being me, then mouth in reply
some shallow or sorry phrase or word
too starved of breath to make itself heard.'

★ GRADE BOOSTER

If you are discussing sound in a poem, always discuss the effect created and link it to the meaning of the poem wherever you can.

But the harmonium can also be seen as a motif for the relationship between father and son. For example, male generations were linked as choristers through the 'gilded finches' of song, and the music of the once vibrant harmonium – a music that contrasts with the lack of communication between the contemporary father and son.

Their relationship, however, is not without its lighter side. The touch of self-pity about the father as he draws attention to his possible demise is gently humorous. This is echoed in the son's response or 'sorry phrase', for although he does not know what to reply to his father, he is also struggling to say anything at all under the weight of the harmonium.

These comic images suggest that the relationship is not in conflict, only lacking in emotional expression (and this gives the poem its emotional impact). So the relationship is also a little sad. It is like the old harmonium. 'One of its notes' has 'lost its tongue', but it can still strike 'a chord'. Though the father and son may not communicate very well, they are together helping each other, and to this extent are in harmony.

MOVING ALONG

The poem is free verse and the rhythm shifts as we read. However, rhythms are repeated, for example in the first and last verse, which are **dipodic**. They have a swaying movement. This helps to carry the poem along. It also gives lightness, contrasting with the awkward, gloomy exchange between father and son and the heavy business of shifting the harmonium.

Rhyme, of which there are several examples, does much the same. Notice the internal rhyme 'flat'/'back' in the final verse, which accentuates the rolling movement of the line. Rhyme can also help link ideas. The rhyme 'freight'/'weight' links the harmonium with the idea of a coffin. It can bring closure too. The **rhyming couplet** at the end brings the poem to a gentle halt.

EXAMINER'S TIP: WRITING ABOUT THE SOUND EFFECTS OF THE POEM

You should also be aware of the techniques used to create subtle sound effects in the poem. Alliteration, particularly the use of the **sibilant** 's' and 'sh', is common. It often gives a soft sound but can also produce a clear, bright sound. For example, it accentuates the brilliance of the image 'Sunlight, through stained glass'.

Perhaps the subtlest sound effects, however, are produced by assonance of which there is a good deal in the poem. The repetition of sound helps to create unity as well as emphasis, as in 'stained', 'saints' and 'raise', or in the repetition of 'a' and 'ar' in the first two lines. This last example also works with 'sh' and 'ch' to add emphasis to the dusty image of the old harmonium in the shadows. As a rule assonance produces harmonious sounds, which is especially appropriate when we consider the title of the poem.

EXAMINER'S TIP

Don't spend too long explaining the events or content of a poem. Discuss the poem's meaning and any effects that emphasise the meaning.

CHECKPOINT 9

Find an example of alliteration in verse three and say how it links to the poem's meaning.

COMPARE THIS POEM WITH . . .

Nettles – about a father protecting his son.

Praise Song for My Mother – a daughter's tribute to her mother.

GLOSSARY

harmonium a keyboard instrument similar to an organ that creates sound using metal reeds rather than pipes

Farrand Chapelette Farrand is the company that makes the Chapelette, a small harmonium

Andrew Forster: 'Brothers'

SUMMARY

① The speaker, a nine-year-old boy, is looking after his younger brother for the afternoon.

② They set off across the field to the bus stop, with the speaker's friend, Paul.

③ The brother realises that he has no bus fare and is told to go home to ask for the money.

④ The bus arrives and the two friends run to catch it.

⑤ The speaker looks back to see his brother in the distance, but runs on without him.

WHAT IS SPECIAL ABOUT THIS POEM?

A The poem is told from the **speaker's perspective** as a nine-year-old boy.
B The theme is the rift between two brothers.
C It is a free verse poem written in two quintains, followed by a quatrain.
D Strong, quirky images depict the **character** of the younger brother.

THE SPEAKER

The adult speaker is telling the poem from the point of view of his younger, nine-year-old self. The voice therefore speaks from a child's perspective but with adult knowledge. The first two verses tell the events as the child might, and the adult voice has prominence in the final verse.

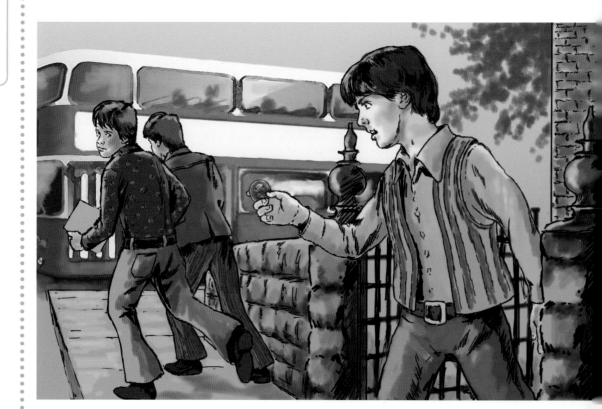

THE RIFT

The rift between the brothers comes to a head in the final verse. The speaker is looking back at his brother as he leaves him behind. But he is also looking back at the past. He sees his brother 'spring towards the gate', his bus fare in his hand, and the image remains in the memory. It implies the guilt the speaker feels at this small betrayal, particularly since the brother's hand is held out, a symbol of friendship. The final line is a metaphor that takes us into the future. A rift has grown between the brothers, and the speaker is unable 'to close the distance' between them.

EXAMINER'S TIP: WRITING ABOUT THE BROTHER

You should note that, of the three boys, the brother is the most fully drawn. Several images evoke a touching innocence. Wearing a fashionable but absurd 'tank-top' and 'spouting six-year-old views', he skips along, delighted to be with the older boys.

The brother's betrayal is therefore all the more potent when it comes, and the reader cannot help but see the child left behind at the gate baffled and hurt. '

CHECKPOINT 10

What does the 'smile' between the speaker and Paul suggest will happen next and why?

COMPARE THIS POEM WITH

Sister Maude – about betrayal between two sisters.
Praise Song for My Mother – a daughter's tribute to her mother.

GLOSSARY

tank top close-fitting sleeveless top

Mimi Khalvati: 'Ghazal'

SUMMARY

① The speaker requests a wished-for lover to woo her.

② The speaker imagines the relationship over time, and how it might end.

WHAT IS SPECIAL ABOUT THIS POEM?

A The poem is an elegant ghazal, a traditional **Persian love poem**.
B Its theme is **unrequited** or **unattainable** love.
C It is written in couplets, with repeated double rhyme and refrain.
D The **poet's name** is **embedded** in the first and last couplet.
E The elaborate **images** are made up of **pairs**.
F The voice is **passionate** and full of **longing**.

UNREQUITED LOVE

What indications are there that the lover is only a would-be lover? In the first couplet there is a desire to be wooed. The same request is a constant refrain expressed in different ways throughout the poem. The repetition of 'If' at the beginning of many lines also suggests that the speaker is imagining a relationship.

But the telling words 'the arms around my bark, arms that never knew me', reinforced by the fervent plea 'Oh would that I were bark!', suggest that the speaker feels a deep longing. The plea is continued in the following couplet in which the speaker asks what they must do to win the loved one. The theme would therefore seem to be unrequited or unobtainable love.

SPEAKING IN PAIRS

The voice passionately explores the different ways the loved one can 'pursue' the speaker and become united. The imagined relationship is also followed to its conclusion, when the speaker and loved one 'are just good friends'.

The intimacy of this imagined relationship is so powerful that we feel the loved one presence, even though they are absent from the poem and we never know their response. Indeed there may be no lover. The poem may be exploring ideal love.

EXAMINER'S TIP: WRITING ABOUT THE POEM'S IMAGES

Note how the images are paired, such as 'the grass' and 'the breeze' or 'the rose' and 'the bird'. Sometimes they are two opposites or halves. These reflect the different positions of the loved one and the unloved speaker that become united and made whole in the poem. Most images are gentle, but some are violent. This is in keeping with the traditional ghazal. The power of love is so great it can 'pierce the heart' or it can 'subdue' the snake's 'venomous tongue'.

KEY QUOTE

'Oh would that I were bark! So old and still in leaf.
And you, dropping in my shade, dew to bedew me!'

KEY CONNECTIONS

The image of the bird and the rose in the poem is reminiscent of Oscar Wilde's fairy story 'The Nightingale and the Rose', in which human love is rejected.

COMPARE THIS POEM WITH . . .

The Farmer's Bride – about unrequited love.
Sonnet 43 – about the quality of true love.

GLOSSARY

Rumi (1207–1273) a great Persian poet and mystic
Shamsuddin wrote an account of Rumi's life

Andrew Marvell: 'To His Coy Mistress'

SUMMARY

- The speaker declares his love to a young woman. She is shy and unyielding.

- He reproaches her light-heartedly, saying that her hesitation would not matter if they had all the time in the world.

- However, youth passes so quickly, he argues, that there should be no delay in expressing their love.

WHAT IS SPECIAL ABOUT THIS POEM?

A   We have a clear sense of the **voice** of the poem, which is written in the first person as the character of a young man.

B   It is structured as an argument in three parts, written in **rhyming couplets** in groups of ten, six and seven.

C   It discusses the **themes** of lust and the shortness of life.

D   It is a **metaphysical poem**. Its style is clever and witty and it uses startling imagery and **hyperbole**.

LIFE IS SHORT

The main theme of the poem is that life is short. Decay and death are the opposites of vigour and youth. They are depicted as ever-present threats offering nothing but 'Deserts of vast eternity'. There is no suggestion that there is a happy afterlife, for this would not serve the aim: to win over the young woman. The only way to defy time is to enjoy the pleasures of youth.

LOVE VERSUS DESIRE

Another theme of the poem would seem to be 'love', but it is more accurate to call it 'desire'. Does the young man swear undying love? Rather he makes fun of love that matures, calling it a 'vegetable love' for its slow growth. He is drawn to physical beauty and a desire to consummate the relationship speedily.

EXAMINER'S TIP: WRITING ABOUT LANGUAGE AND TECHNIQUE

Discuss the effects of the startling imagery, such as the absurd image, in the last couplet of the first part, for although 'none … embrace', in the grave that is exactly what the reader sees, two skeletons fondly embracing. The cadence and rhyme allow the couplet to trip off the tongue, like a witty expression, and reinforce the idea that to wait for love is foolish.

Progress and revision check

REVISION ACTIVITY

1 Which poem is about a daughter's love for her mother? (Write your answers below)

....

2 Which poem is about renewing a relationship after war?

....

3 Why is the speaker so joyful in 'Hour'?

....

4 In which poem is the speaker looking back at his relationship with his brother?

....

5 Which poem is about a father's concern for his small son?

....

REVISION ACTIVITY

On a piece of paper write down answers to these questions:

● What argument does the speaker use to persuade a young woman to accept his love in 'To His Coy Mistress'? *The argument the speaker uses to persuade the young woman to accept his love is that …*

● Why does the speaker wish that the newborn baby in 'Born Yesterday' should be ordinary? *The speaker wishes that the baby should be ordinary because …*

GRADE BOOSTER

In what ways are love and violence connected in Carol Ann Duffy's poem 'Quickdraw'? Think about:

● the way the speaker describes her feelings

● the images that are used.

For a C grade: Convey your ideas clearly and appropriately (you could use words from the question to guide your answer) and refer to details from the poem (use specific examples).

For an A grade: Make sure you comment on the varied ways that love is described, and if possible come up with your own original or alternative ideas.

Also, comment on the effect of particular language choices, exploring a wide range of connotations and links.

Key contexts

RENAISSANCE POETRY

The Renaissance in England was a time of great cultural and artistic flowering. It spanned the reigns of Elizabeth I and James I (VI of Scotland) and beyond.

In Shakespeare's time power lay with the monarch and the court. For example, poetry was often written for Queen Elizabeth or with her ideal in mind, since she was perceived as a godlike figure. Several different verse forms also developed, such as the Shakespearean sonnet. During Marvell's time power was shifting and there was great political unrest, especially during the Civil War when Charles I was beheaded.

Shakespeare's sonnets were probably composed at different times and Shakespeare may have written them for a private audience. But he would have known the courtly conventions well and would have been conscious of any changes he made to the traditional sonnet. Andrew Marvell was a metaphysical poet. He also wrote satires – some were too dangerous to be published. 'To His Coy Mistress' is also bold and witty, and uses argument rather than flattery.

VICTORIAN BELIEF

The Victorian period is often referred to as the 'age of doubt', when religious faith was questioned particularly in the wake of Darwin's theories of evolution. Some people turned to new forms of Christian belief or spiritualism, and various sects sprang up. Christianity was also closely linked to a middle-class view of social responsibility, and many believed that it was their duty to reform or help others.

Both Elizabeth Barrett Browning and Christina Rossetti were religous and were involved in issues of social justice. For the former poetry was a kind of spirituality, and we could think of 'Sonnet 43' as a hymn to love. For Christina Rossetti religion was all-encompassing and most of her work has Christian imagery. Christian morality is also present in 'Sister Maude', with its concern for the soul and with issues of good and evil.

CULTURAL INFLUENCES

English poets have always borrowed forms from other cultures. For example, the well-known Japanese haiku has been reworked in English to produce the English haiku, in which the strict syllable form is not always used.

KEY CONNECTIONS

Shakespeare's 'Sonnet 18' featured in a *Dr Who* episode, 'The Shakespearean Code', broadcast in April 2007.

? DID YOU KNOW?

Shakespeare's sonnets are truly global. They have been translated into every major language and many languages less widely spoken.

? DID YOU KNOW?

Charlotte Mew lived across two centuries. Her poems explore nineteenth-century concerns, such as the nature of religious belief, but are often written in a modern style.

Both the **praise song** and the **ghazal** are not English forms, and the poets Mimi Khalvati and Grace Nichols have diverse cultural experience. However, they both write in English, adapting the forms to suit the language or the poet's personal design. For example, in the traditional ghazal the same words are repeated at the end of each couplet. In 'Ghazal' the words differ, though the sound is the same. Praise songs are often written for public occasions and performed by musicians. 'Praise Song for my Mother' is an intimate personal tribute.

KEY CONNECTIONS

Vernon Scannell's experience of war had a deep effect on him, and themes of violence and death often occur in his poetry, as they do in 'Nettles'.

EXAMINER'S TIP: WRITING ABOUT CONTEXT

The period in which a writer is writing will affect their work. For example, poets writing during the First or Second World War produced poetry that was greatly affected by war and its consequences. Sometimes a period has a less obvious influence. Writers who cross two centuries may produce work that has aspects of both. Always find out about a writer's period and culture to gain insight into their writing. If you wish to discuss it in the exam, make sure it is part of your commentary on the poem and not simply added on. For example, when discussing the poem 'Nettles', we might say: *All the most powerful images are associated with war, something that the poet had direct experience of and which deeply affected him.*

Key themes

TRUE LOVE

Two poems in particular, 'Sonnet 43' and 'Sonnet 116', explore the meaning of true love. They do this is different ways. A third, 'Laura's poem: The Manhunt', explores the struggle to renew love.

Elizabeth Barrett Browning's **sonnet** is a celebration of a love that is not in doubt. It attempts to understand a deep personal love felt for another. Shakespeare's sonnet possesses a similar certainty, but sees true love in the abstract, without a lover in mind. Love is an 'ever-fixed mark' and does not 'alter', regardless of how it is tested. The ultimate test in both poems is time, and each sees true love as capable of transcending life.

GRADE BOOSTER

If the rhythm of a poem doesn't seem to suit the theme, ask yourself: why has the poet created this conflict?

'Laura's poem: The Manhunt' shares the same depth of feeling as the sonnets, but here a profound change of circumstances has taken place. The poem describes how intimate love is being relearned through a struggle to understand the effects of wa on the loved one.

REVISION ACTIVITY

Here are examples from the cluster that share this theme. Are there any others?

- Elizabeth Barrett Browning: 'Sonnet 43'
- William Shakespeare: 'Sonnet 116'
- Simon Armitage: 'Laura's poem: The Manhunt'

BREAKDOWN AND BETRAYAL

love's constancy is the **theme** of some poems, hen breakdown and suffering is the theme of thers. In 'The Farmer's Bride', breakdown occurs ecause the farmer's expectations of his marriage ome to nothing. His frightened wife cowers at is touch, and both suffer because they are nable to overcome their difficulties.

uffering is also present in 'Sister Maude'. Here he breakdown between two sisters comes in the hape of betrayal – a betrayal so bitter that the elationship cannot be mended. Sister Maude has ecome an outcast, biding 'with death and sin'. 'Quickdraw', the reader is witness to the reakdown. The relationship is blasted apart, estroyed by a symbolic gun.

hough they are very different in style, each poem leaves us with the same feeling: at the relationship is beyond hope, ruling out any possibility of new beginnings.

REVISION ACTIVITY

Here are examples from the cluster that share this theme. Are there any others?

- Charlotte Mew: 'The Farmer's Bride'
- Christina Rossetti: 'Sister Maude'
- Carol Ann Duffy: 'Quickdraw'

DESIRE

esire or lust runs through several poems in the cluster. Poems such as 'Hour' escribe the intensity of desire in a love affair. 'Ghazal' explores an experience as tense, but one that takes place in the imagination. Desire is also present in 'The armer's Bride', with sinister overtones, as the farmer yearns for relations with an nwilling wife.

he poem 'In Paris with You' is much lighter in tone. The speaker seems able to vercome hurt pride with the prospect of a new love and the chance of new leasures. Following your desires is also a theme in 'To His Coy Mistress'. But heming is evident here, as the speaker attempts to inveigle his way into the fections of a young woman.

KEY CONNECTIONS

Elizabeth Barrett Browning's most accomplished work is her epic poem *Aurora Leigh*, in which the heroine achieves an independent life as a writer, while also finding love on her own terms.

KEY CONNECTIONS

Carol Ann Duffy's collection *Rapture* details the course of a love affair from beginning to end. Both 'Hour' and 'Quickdraw' come from the collection. You can think about the relationship between these poems and where each comes in the collection.

KEY CONNECTIONS

Agha Shahid Ali compiled an important anthology of ghazals in English, *Ravishing Disunities: Real Ghazals in English*, published by Wesleyan (2000).

REVISION ACTIVITY

Here are examples from the cluster that share this theme. Are there any others?

● Carol Ann Duffy: 'Hour'
● James Fenton: 'In Paris with You'
● Andrew Marvell: 'To His Coy Mistress"

FAMILY BONDS

Family relationships, whether cause for celebration or regret, feature in several poems and cover a variety of emotions. For example, the depth of the love felt for the mother in 'Praise Song for My Mother' contrasts strongly with the hatred felt for the sister in 'Sister Maude'.

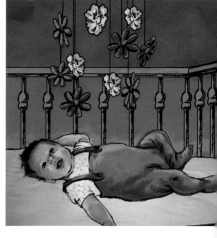

The father's urge to protect his son against life's trials in 'Nettles' is a feeling most parents can identify with. In 'Born Yesterday', there is no parental bond. But the birth of a friend's child also evokes protective feelings in the speaker as he wishes her true happiness.

Conversely, the sense of regret in 'Brothers' at the speaker's poor treatment of his younger brother makes the title of the poem poignant and **ironic**. Brotherhood after all means love and loyalty. There is poignancy in 'Harmonium' in the relationship between father and son as they struggle to communicate while also carrying the harmonium. Nonetheless, the reader senses an underlying bond. In many of the relationships depicted in the poems love is the bond that is either nurtured or broken.

GRADE BOOSTER

Remember all the poems in *Relationships* are about love or the lack of it. But the emotions expressed are diverse. To help you identify these feelings ask yourself questions about each poem. Are the feelings serious, intense or light-hearted? Do the feelings change? Find images that describe the speaker's or character's experience and commit some to memory. You can refer to them in the exam.

REVISION ACTIVITY

Here are examples from the cluster that share this theme. Are there any others?

● Andrew Forster: 'Brothers'
● Grace Nichols: 'Praise Song for My Mother'
● Christina Rossetti: 'Sister Maude'

Progress and revision check

REVISION ACTIVITY

1. Which sonnet is set in the Elizabethan period and who wrote it? (Write your answers below)

....

2. Which poems are set in the nineteenth century?

....

3. Name a poem whose theme is betrayal.

....

4. What do you think is the main theme of 'In Paris With You'?

....

5. What are two themes of 'To His Coy Mistress'?

....

REVISION ACTIVITY

On a piece of paper write down answers to these questions:

- Which poems suggest that the poets are concerned about war and its consequences, and how? *The poems that are concerned with war are … This is revealed …*

- What happens to time, and why, in Carol Ann Duffy's poem 'Hour'? *In 'Hour' time seems to …… because …...*

GRADE BOOSTER

What happens in the final verse of 'Brothers' and how does it reveal the relationship between the brothers? Think about:

- where each brother is and what they are doing

  what the last line tells us.

For a C grade: describe clearly the events and how you think each brother feels (you could use words from the question to guide your answer). Also say what this means for their relationship.

For an A grade: comment on the different perspectives of each brother and show how the events imply the future relationship between them, linking this to the theme.

Focus on inferences that can be drawn from what is not said or how language choices create a particular tone or voice.

PART FOUR: LANGUAGE AND STRUCTURE

Here are some useful terms to know when writing about the cluster, what they mea[n] and examples from the poems.

Literary term	Means?	Example
allusion	a reference in a work of literature to something outside the work, such as poetry, fiction myth, historical or biographical detail	In 'Hour' the speaker refers to a 'Midas' light, an allusion to the Greek myth of King Midas, whose touch turned everything to gold.
ambiguity	when words or sentences have more than one meaning and it is not clear which is the true interpretation	In the final line of 'Laura's poem: The Manhunt', we cannot be sure what Laura 'comes close' to. Is it love, pity, understanding, intimacy or all of these?
caesura	a pause during a line of poetry to create an effect	In Shakespeare's 'Sonnet 116' the pause in the middle of the second line gives weight to the words that follow: 'Love is not love …'. (They in turn run into the next line, to emphasise love's constancy. See enjambment below.)
enjambment	when a line runs on into the next without pause, sometimes called 'run-on line'	In the third verse of 'Quickdraw' line 2 runs into line 3 and carries with it the idea that love is falling apart: '… calamity, hard liquor / in the old Last Chance saloon …'
personification	when things or ideas are treated as if they were people, with human attributes and feelings	Throughout the poem 'Nettles', the plants are treated as if they were soldiers in a war, fighting with 'green spears' and inflicting 'sharp wounds'.

EXAMINER'S TIP

Write down in a notebook a few literary terms such as image, metaphor and simile with examples next to them. Commit them to memory and remember the differences between them when referring to language in the exam.

NATURE IMAGERY

Imagery is used to bring ideas to life by appealing to our feelings and senses, mos[t] often the sense of sight. As soon as we meet an image in a poem, a picture comes t[o] mind.

Varieties of nature imagery can be found in many poems in the cluster, and of thes[e] metaphor and simile are the most common. Larkin uses a flower bud as a metapho[r] for the new baby in 'Born Yesterday'. In 'To his Coy Mistress', 'the 'youthful hue' sit[s]

n the lover's skin 'like morning dew'. Nature is used to depict the mother in 'Praise ong for My Mother' and to conjure desire and longing in 'Ghazal'. The imagined overs, for example, come together as 'the grass' and 'the breeze'.

ometimes nature provides the backdrop, as 'the summer sky and a grass ditch' do in Hour'. But in whatever way nature is used in these poems, all the images link to uman relationships. This is most fully realised in 'The Farmer's Bride', where nature rovides the setting, as well as the **similes** that describe the young wife.

he farmer in the final verses laments the coming of winter and the shortening days, s 'One leaf in the still air falls slowly down', an image we associate with his ill-arred relationship.

CREATING A CHARACTER

character in a poem is usually depicted through the imagery. For example, we see e small son crying in 'Nettles' after his 'tender skin' has been stung. Or we see the x-year-old at the beginning of 'Brothers' as happy-go-lucky, chatting about otherham United'.

he images created are seen through the eyes of the speaker. Even a single word uggesting their attitude can intensify the picture of a character. In 'Nettles' a word ch as 'soothed' tells us that the child is loved and cared for, and able to offer watery grin' when comforted.

'Brothers' the voice is annoyed rather than concerned. The first words of the oem, 'Saddled with you', suggest the speaker's irritation at having to look after his ounger brother. When he goes on to depict him wearing a 'ridiculous tank-top', we nile at the image, but at the same time recognise the contempt in the voice. It tells s that the speaker is embarrassed by his brother's presence and would rather he ere not there. This increased knowledge makes the poem's final image of the jected six-year-old all the sadder.

EVERYDAY WORDS

he language used by the speaker or a character will help to create the poem's ood, which might be comic or light-hearted, thoughtful or serious. Sometimes a oet will choose everyday language or a dialect to build a particular atmosphere or eate a character.

mon Armitage is well known for including **colloquial** language in his poetry. In armonium' the everyday expressions 'bundled off' and 'cart it away' accentuate e harmonium's sorry state. They also contrast skilfully with the **figurative** nguage depicting the instrument as it once was, when its 'hummed harmonics' companied the choristers. Similarly, the speaker in 'Born Yesterday' uses everyday pressions when chatting to the baby that contrast with the rich, soaring adjectives scribing happiness in the final verse.

Paris With You' is notable for its everyday speech and slang. It gives the speaker a iful, comic **tone**. Though wounded in love and tired of hearing about it, he can't lp but talk of it. **Dialect** dominates 'The Farmer's Bride'. Swapping the pronouns

EXAMINER'S TIP

If you are answering a question on a narrative poem, don't retell the whole story. Be aware of the **theme** and some key images that relate to it.

EXAMINER'S TIP

Time yourself when answering a question. Remember you have other questions to answer and you can only get a certain number of marks for each one.

EXAMINER'S TIP

Don't confuse literary terms, such as **simile** and **metaphor**. If you're not sure what they mean, don't use them. Just write about the effect the language creates when you read the poem.

KEY CONNECTIONS

What we call the Shakespearean sonnet did not begin with Shakespeare! Sir Philip Sidney wrote a sonnet sequence, *Astrophel* and *Stella*, that took the **Petrarchan sonnet** and adapted it in the 1580s.

EXAMINER'S TIP

If you enjoy a poem written by a particular poet, read more of their work. It will give you further insights into their style that you might find useful in the exam.

'us' and 'we' and using the contractions ''twasn't' and ''mong' and expressions such as 'up-along' and 'men-folk' signify a rustic dialect. They also tell us the farmer is an ordinary countryman who sees the world and his circumstances through rural eyes.

SHIFTS AND MOVEMENTS

A poem's structure refers to the arrangements of the words on the page and to the way the poem unfolds through its rhythm and movement. Most importantly, the structure will in some way relate to the **theme** and help create mood. The bouncing jaunty rhythm of 'In Paris with You' is important in telling us that the speaker is not destroyed by his unhappy love affair. On the contrary, he is happy to begin another.

The forms of 'Sonnet 43' and 'Sonnet 116' follow traditional patterns. Typically, a **sonnet** begins with a problem or idea, which is then explored until a resolution is reached. 'To His Coy Mistress' presents an argument in three parts, in which the pace increases until the speaker with a flourish concludes his argument for seizing opportunity 'Through the iron gates of life'.

Free verse poems also have their movements. The leisurely opening of 'Born Yesterday' belies the exhilarating final movement that depicts the achievement of true happiness. The stops and starts in 'Quickdraw' suit the images of the lovers as they hurl insults down the phone.

EXAMINER'S TIP: WRITING ABOUT LANGUAGE AND THEME

Sometimes you will need to search for meaning in the **imagery** and make connections between the images to discover the theme. Take the first line of 'Quickdraw'. What clues are there to the poem's meaning? 'Phones' are 'like guns', which indicates anger and violence. We can also guess that this is to do with a relationship, since we use phones to communicate. When the phone rings, the voice at the other end is harsh, like 'a pellet', and the speaker groans. So the relationship is in trouble. In the second verse, the first line is a clear statement, 'You've wounded me', that describes hurt feelings. From here we read the tongue is a 'trigger', the heart is 'blast[ed]' and love is 'calamity'. We can follow the imagery from anger to cruelty to understand the theme as the breakdown of the relationship.

So when studying a poem, trace the images and words from the beginning; consider what they suggest and how they link to what happens in the poem. This should help you identify the theme or themes.

Progress and revision check

REVISION ACTIVITY

1. In which poem is a young woman compared to 'the first wild violets'? (Write your answers below

   ....

2. What views is the six-year-old expressing in 'Brothers'?

   ....

3. In which poem is a shoulder blade a 'fractured rudder' and a lung 'parachute silk'?

   ....

4. Which four poems have the names of particular forms of poetry in their titles?

   ....

5. How would you describe the rhythm of 'In Paris with You'?

   ....

REVISION ACTIVITY

On a piece of paper write down answers to these questions:

- What aspects of nature does the poet use to describe the mother in 'Praise Song for My Mother'?
  The aspects of nature the speaker uses to describe the mother are …

- In what state is the harmonium, and how is it depicted, in 'Harmonium'?
  The state of the harmonium is depicted …

GRADE BOOSTER

How are the nettles portrayed in the poem 'Nettles' and in what way do they link to the speaker's son? Think about:

- the images used to depict the nettles

- the speaker's need to protect his son.

For a C grade: make sure you discuss what the images mean (you could use words from the question to guide your answer) and how their meaning links to the speaker's son (refer to specific examples).

For an A grade: make sure you show how the images link to each other, referring to some of the literary techniques used to create them. Also make sure you show the link between the images and the speaker's son and what the effect on the reader might be.

PART FIVE: GRADE BOOSTER

Understanding the question

Questions in exams or controlled conditions often need **'decoding'**. Decoding the question helps to ensure that your answer will be relevant and refers to what you have been asked.

 UNDERSTAND EXAM LANGUAGE

Get used to exam and essay-style language by looking at specimen questions and the words they use. For example:

Exam speak!	Means?	Example: 'Praise Song for My Mother'
'convey ideas'	*'get across a point to the reader'* Usually you have to say *'how'* this is done.	The depiction of the mother as fishes' gills *conveys* the idea of the breath of life.
'methods, techniques, ways'	The *'things'* the writer does – such as a powerful description, introducing a shocking event, how someone speaks, etc.	The poet uses *metaphor* as a *technique* to depict the mother as water's depth, suggesting she has insight.
'present, represent'	1) present: *'the ways things are told to us'* 2) represent: *'what those things might mean underneath'*	The writer *presents* the reader with depictions of the mother. They could *represent* the idea of nurture.

 'BREAK DOWN' THE QUESTION

Pick out the **key words** or phrases. For example:

> Question: '**Compare** how the **theme** of **desire** is depicted in **'Hour'** and **one other poem** from *Relationships*.

- The focus is on **'the theme (main idea) of desire (wanting or longing for something)'**, which means you will have to say what kind of desire is depicted in the poem, and do the same for the depiction of desire in another poem.

- The word **'compare'** means that you must look at both the similarities and the differences in the portrayal of desire in the poems.

What does this tell you?

When discussing the **theme** you must decide how **language** is used to convey the feelings and wants of the characters or speakers.

 KNOW YOUR LITERARY LANGUAGE!

When studying texts you will come across words such as 'theme, issue, idea', 'symbol', 'imagery', 'metaphor', etc. Some of these words could come up in the question you are asked. Make sure you know what they mean before you write your answer!

Comparing poems

Comparing poems is a **key skill** which requires **careful thought**. Some of the skills you need are general ones, useful for any comparison work; others are specific to poetry.

When comparing **two** poems, you will need to:

● Comment on **points of similarity** and **points of difference**.

● Write about the **overall subject** of the **question** (i.e. the theme of conflict) but **focus** on the **different aspects** of **each poem** (language, structure, voice, etc.).

● Write in a **logical, structured way** that makes your ideas **clear** and **easy to follow** (use linking words and phrases, such as 'but' and 'however', to guide the examiner through what you say).

● Try to come up with your own **individual interpretation** or thoughts.

HOW TO START: A GOOD INTRODUCTION

You could begin with a general introduction comparing the two poems. For example:

> The poems 'Sonnet 43' and 'Laura's Poem: The Manhunt' depict **different experiences of love** through their **structure**, **themes** and **language**.

This introduction then gives you the chance to deal with **each of these aspects** in turn.

DEVELOPING THE COMPARISON: WRITE A PARAGRAPH FOR EACH POINT

Here is an example, in which the same point is explored in regard to both poems:

> As the name suggests, 'Sonnet 43' uses a common **structure** for a love poem, the sonnet. It is a celebration of how the speaker's feelings encompass 'the depth and breadth and height' of the soul. The love that is felt is expressed openly and freely. **By comparison**, 'Laura's Poem: The Manhunt' expresses in free verse a love that must be renewed in small steps. The repetition throughout the poem of 'only then' suggests that the speaker must tread carefully because her soldier-lover has been physically and mentally damaged by war.

First sentence introduces the idea that this paragraph will deal with this aspect

Comparative term links both poems

PERSONAL INTERPRETATION

You can add your own views at any point, but the key is to think **'outside the box'**. For example, you *could* say: 'It is possible that the poet wants to describe the way that war not only damages the soldier physically and mentally but also affects relationships.'

AQA Poetry Anthology: Relationships **45**

> **EXAMINER'S TIP**
>
> Dealing in turn with each aspect in both poems, is a high-level skill which will show your ability to compare and contrast. If this is too challenging, you can write about *each poem in turn*, but you must make comparative and contrasting comments as you go along.

Dealing with an 'unseen' poem

This aspect of the written exam may seem daunting. But it is an opportunity to show off your **creative thinking** and **analytical skills**.

 ## ADAPT TO SURVIVE

Normally, you would be able to **annotate** a poem (underline key words, write questions, highlight phrases, etc.) but in the written exam *you are not allowed to do this*. The instructions state:

- Do not annotate the poems.
- Write any rough work in your answer book.
- Cross out anything you don't wish to be marked.

This is fine. All you need to do is:

- Read the poem in the exam paper once or twice without writing anything.
- Then, write notes about the poem in your answer book.
- Put a heading 'Notes' so that you know to cross these out later.

 ## KEEP IT SIMPLE!

- Start your notes by quickly jotting down what you think the 'story' of the poem is. This could be as simple as: 'the poet talks about a river and what he sees' or, 'the poet expresses her feelings about her son.'
- Then, as you would if you were annotating the poem itself, jot down *very quickly* the key things you notice about:

❶ The **structure** (verses, patterns, repetitions, rhyme/sound, etc.).

❷ Key powerful **words/phrases** (don't write them out, just put a line reference – e.g. line 2: strong metaphor).

❸ Anything related to the question itself (does it mention a **theme** or **idea**?).

Don't take any more than five minutes for this. You **only have 30 minutes** for the whole answer.

 ## STICK TO WHAT THE POET DOES AND THE EFFECT

Almost certainly your question will be about how the poet *presents* an idea, so in your answer think of making 4–5 points about how the poet makes his point, presents his idea, tells his story. One point for each paragraph.

 **EXAMINER'S TIP**

The lover of 'To His Coy Mistress' explains that if they had 'but world enough and time' for courtship, the lady's shyness would not matter. This is a clever device to suggest that his mistress certainly deserves praise of this magnitude, but life is against them so it's not his fault that he's hurrying her!

Planning your answer

t is vital that you plan your response to the controlled assessment task or possible xam question carefully, and that you then follow your plan, if you are to gain the igher grades.

 ## ANNOTATE AND ORGANISE

Vhen revising for the exam, or planning your response to the controlled assessment ask, make **notes** on particular aspects of the poems you have highlighted, so that ou have a **'ready reference'** for comparison, revision or planning purposes. For xample, you might list ideas as shown below for the poem 'Brothers':

Key point/aspect	Evidence (quotation, reference to structure, etc.)	The effect this has or the idea conveyed
the poem is told n the voice of a child, but with adult knowledge	'and we must stroll the town doing what grown-ups do'	conveys the idea that the child-speaker needs to feel important

 ## PLAN FOR PARAGRAPHS

se paragraphs to plan your answer.

The first paragraph should **introduce** the **argument** you wish to make.

Then, jot down how the paragraphs that follow will **develop** this argument with **details**, **examples** and other possible **points of view**. Each paragraph is likely to deal with one point at a time.

Sum up your argument in the last paragraph.

or example, for the following task:

QUESTION: Compare how attitudes to family relationships are shown in 'Brothers' nd one other poem from *Relationships*.

Simple plan:
Paragraph 1: Introduction
Paragraph 2: First point – *explore attitudes to family relationships in 'Brothers', e.g. about the irritation felt by the child-speaker at having to look after his younger brother*
Paragraph 3: Second point – *further comment on attitudes in 'Brothers', e.g. about the young brother's delight at being with the older boys*
Paragraph 4: Third point – *explore attitudes to same theme/issue in other poem from the cluster*
Paragraph 5: Fourth point – *make new point about attitudes to theme/issue in the other poem*
Paragraph 6: Conclusion – *draw together what you want to say about the theme across the two poems*

EXAMINER'S TIP

Where appropriate refer to the language technique used and the effect it creates. For example, if you say 'this metaphor shows how ...' or 'the effect of this metaphor is to emphasise to the reader ...' this will get you much higher marks.

How to use quotations

One of the secrets of success in writing essays is to use quotations **effectively**. There are five basic principles:

1 Put quotation marks at the beginning and end of the quotation.

2 Write the quotation exactly as it appears in the original.

3 Do not use a quotation that repeats what you have just written.

4 Use the quotation so that it fits into your sentence, or if it is longer, indent it as a separate paragraph.

5 Only quote what is most useful.

 USE QUOTATIONS TO DEVELOP YOUR ARGUMENT

Quotations should be used to develop the line of thought in your essays. Your comment should not duplicate what is in your quotation. For example …

EXAMINER'S TIP

Try using a quotation to begin your response. You can use it as a launch-pad for your ideas, or as an idea you are going to argue against.

GRADE D/E

(simply repeats the idea)
The lover of 'To His Coy Mistress' explains that if they had all the time in the world for him to court her, the lady's shyness would not matter. He says: 'Had we but world enough, and time, This coyness, Lady, were no crime'.

GRADE C

(makes a point and supports it with a relevant quotation)
The lover of 'To His Coy Mistress' explains that the lady's shyness at being courted would not matter if they had 'but world enough and time'.

However, the most sophisticated way of using the writer's words is to embed them into your sentence, and further develop the point:

GRADE A

(makes point, embeds quote and develops idea)
The lover of 'To His Coy Mistress' explains that if they had 'but world enough and time' for courtship, the lady's shyness would not matter. This is a clever device to suggest that his mistress certainly deserves praise of this magnitude, but life is against them so it's not his fault that he's hurrying her!

When you use quotations in this way, you are demonstrating the ability to use text as evidence to support your ideas – not simply including words from the original to prove you have read it.

Sitting the examination

Examination papers are carefully designed to give you the opportunity to do your best. Follow these handy hints for exam success.

 BEFORE YOU START

- Make sure that you **know the poems** you are writing about so that you are properly prepared and equipped. If you are preparing for an **'unseen'** poem, make sure you have **practised** relevant **techniques** to succeed.

- You need to be **comfortable** and **free from distractions**. Inform the invigilator if anything is off-putting, e.g. a shaky desk.

- **Read** and follow the instructions, or rubric, on the front of the examination paper. You should know by now what you need to do but **check** to reassure yourself.

- Before beginning your answer have a **skim** through the **whole paper** to make sure you don't miss anything **important**.

- Observe the **time allocation** – and follow it carefully. If the paper recommends 45 minutes for a particular question on a text make sure this is how long you spend.

 WRITING YOUR RESPONSES

A typical 45 minutes examination essay is between 550 and 800 words in length.

Ideally, spend a minimum of 5 minutes planning your answer before you begin.

Use the questions to structure your response. Here is an example:

Question: Compare how the theme of desire is depicted in 'Hour' and **one** other poem from *Relationships*.

- The introduction to your answer could briefly describe **the two poems** and the 'story' they tell;

- the second part could explain the nature of desire in 'Hour ' and how it is created;

- the third part could explore the **voice in the second poem** you select, possibly linking back to 'Hour'.

- the conclusion would **sum up your own viewpoint**, mentioning the key aspects of each poem.

For each part allocate paragraphs to cover the points you wish to make (see **Planning your answer**). Keep your writing legible and easy to read, using paragraphs and link words to show the structure of your answers. Spend a couple of minutes afterwards quickly checking for obvious errors.

 'KEY WORDS' ARE THE KEY!

Keep on mentioning the **key words** from the question in your answer. This will keep you on track and remind the examiner that you are answering the question set.

> **EXAMINER'S TIP**
>
> Think carefully about how you will answer a question before you begin to write. Ask yourself: What will follow on from the first point I make? What will the next point be after that?

Sitting the controlled assessment

It may be the case that you are responding to 'Ghazal' in a controlled assessment situation. Follow these useful tips for success.

 ## WHAT YOU ARE REQUIRED TO DO

Make sure you are clear about:

- The **specific text** and **task** you are preparing (is it just a poem or poems from this cluster or others?).
- How **long** you have during the assessment period (i.e. 3–4 hours?).
- How **much** you are expected or allowed to write (i.e. 2,000 words).
- **What** you are allowed to **take** into the controlled assessment, and what you can use (or not, as the case may be). You may be able to take in brief notes BUT NOT draft answers, so check with your teacher.

 ## HOW YOU CAN PREPARE

Once you know your task, topic and text/s you can:

- Make **notes** and **prepare** the **points**, **evidence**, **quotations**, etc. you are likely to use.
- Practise or draft **model answers**.
- Use these **York Notes** to hone your **skills** such as use of quotations, how to plan an answer and focus on what makes a **top grade**.

 ## DURING THE CONTROLLED ASSESSMENT

Remember:

- **Stick** to the topic and **task** you have been given.
- The allocated **time** is for **writing**, so make the most of it. It is double the time you might have in an exam, so you will be writing almost **twice as much** (or more) although you *may* also be writing on a larger number of poems, probably at least **four**.
- At the end of the controlled assessment follow your **teacher's instructions**. For example, make sure you have written your **name** clearly on all the pages you hand in.

Improve your grade

t is useful to know the type of responses examiners are looking for when they award different grades. The following broad guidance should help you to improve your grade when responding to the task you are set!

GRADE C

What you need to show	What this means
Sustained response to task and text	You write enough! You don't run out of ideas after two paragraphs.
Effective use of **details** to **support your explanations**	You generally support what you say with evidence, e.g. *The mother in 'Praise Song for My Mother', who provides food such as 'the crab's leg and 'fried plantain', also nourishes through her maternal care, 'replenishing replenishing'.*
Explanation of effects of writer's **use of language,** structure, form, etc. and **effect on readers**	You must write about the writer's use of these things. It's not enough simply to give a viewpoint. So, you might comment on the way a poet uses a final couplet to emphasise a point, or a powerful image to stress an idea, such as the simile of a young wife as 'the first wild violets', representing youth.
Appropriate comment on **characters**, **plots**, **themes**, **ideas** and **settings**	Your comments should relate to the question. If you are asked to write about a character's nature, you should do just that.

GRADE A

What you need to show *in addition* **to the above**	What this means
Insightful, exploratory response to the text	You look for hidden meanings. For example, you might explore how hurt the speaker really is by love in the poem 'In Paris with You', since the lively rhythm might suggest that his heart is easily mended by the prospect of a new love.
Close analysis and use of **detail**	When discussing the way language is used, you might discuss, for example, the number of metaphors used to depict the nettles in the poem 'Nettles'. Their association with war, as 'a regiment of spite' or 'a fierce parade' of soldiers, build to create a motif about suffering in life as well as the pain suffered from the nettles.
Convincing and **imaginative interpretation**	Your viewpoint is likely to convince the examiner. You show you have 'engaged' with the text, and come up with your own ideas. These may be based on what you have discussed in class or read about, but you have made your own decisions.

Annotated sample answers

This section will provide you with extracts from two model answers, one at **C grade** and one at **A grade**, to give you an idea of what is required to achieve at different levels.

> **Question:** Compare the ways poets present the breakdown of a relationship in 'Quickdraw' and one other poem from *Relationships*.

CANDIDATE 1

Quote embedded in the sentence, but could have mentioned the literary technique 'simile'

Point supported by evidence

Good point but needs supporting evidence

Understands what the quotation conveys

Useful comment on the relevance of the berries but doesn't say how they are connected to 'children' and 'Christmas'

When 'Quickdraw' opens we are told that the speaker is carrying two phones 'like guns'. The phone rings. The speaker's lover at the other end talks harshly so that the speaker is 'wounded'. Using guns to describe what is happening suggests that the relationship is angry and violent.

As the quarrel builds up it is like a gunfight because we are told that the tongue is 'a trigger' and the speaker is blasted 'through the heart'. From the way the speaker and lover are behaving it looks as though the relationship is breaking down. There is also a lot of stopping and starting in the middle of lines and this makes the poem jumpy as the two shout insults down the phone.

By the end the speaker has been the most hurt. It is like the ending of a gunfight as if the lover was firing bullets. The speaker seems to fall on their knees as if they were upset. From this we can guess the relationship is over.

Like 'Quickdraw', 'The Farmer's Bride' is also about a broken relationship. The farmer has married a young wife who does not love him. She is very shy. We are told she is 'all in a shiver and a scare'. She is especially frightened of men.

There is no violence between the farmer and his wife like in 'Quickdraw', but there is no companionship either. One of the saddest parts is when the farmer describes his unhappy marriage in autumn and then winter. Nothing is growing except red berries and they remind the farmer that he has no children, especially at Christmas time.

Then at the end we see how awful the relationship is between the farmer and his wife. The farmer watches his wife asleep in her attic bed. He looks at 'The soft young down of her', and we can tell that he wants her badly. This makes us nervous. We feel uneasy at what he might do.

Interprets the poem's opening correctly

Explanation of the poet's use of structure

Correct to make a comparison between the two poems but needs to expand

Good interpretation of the underlying feeling at the end of the poem

---

Overall comment: In general a good understanding of the poems, with suitable evidence including quotations to support some points. Some comparison has been made between the two poems, but further links could have been made. There could also have been more said about the relationship between autumn, winter and the marriage in 'The Farmer's Bride'. Overall a competent answer.

GRADE C

CANDIDATE 2

Shows insight – linking the opening images to a Western

Uses literary term correctly

Convincing interpretation but could discuss more on the build-up in verse three

Close analysis and convincing interpretation of metaphor. Also shows how it contrasts

From the beginning of 'Quickdraw' the speaker is ready for a fight. Two phones are 'slung … from the hips', reminiscent of a gunslinger in a Western. When the lover rings, their voice is 'a pellet' and the speaker's tongue is a 'trigger'. Words are used to cause pain and the reader becomes quickly aware that they are witnessing the breakdown of a relationship, the theme of the poem.

The breakdown is also revealed in the movement of the poem. There are abrupt stops in the middle of lines. There is also enjambment and in verses two and three the lines even run into the next verse. This creates a disjointed rhythm reminding us of the rapid action of a gunfight.

As the poem moves towards the climax in the 'Last Chance saloon', love is all but destroyed. The final verse is like a shoot-out. The relationship is in its death throes as the speaker staggers and the lover, who has the upper hand, fires the decisive words, 'Take this … / and this … and this … and this … and this …'.

If 'Quickdraw' depicts a relationship being destroyed, the 'Farmer's Bride' depicts one that is broken from the outset. It is a marriage that has never been consummated. The poem is told through the farmer's eyes as his expectations of married life dwindle. His young wife, as 'Shy as a leveret', withdraws from the world of humans especially 'men-folk'. She is happier being with animals with whom she has an affinity.

Unlike 'Quickdraw' there is no anger expressed between the wife and husband and little communication. Indeed the husband has hardly heard his wife 'speak at all'. He views the marriage against the seasons, mainly autumn's 'grey sky' and winter's barren 'black earth'. The berries that 'redden up to Christmas-time', a metaphor for sexual experience and fertility, are contrasted with their childlessness.

At the end of the poem, however, the farmer's longing for physical contact takes on a sinister note and here the poem comes closer to Quickdraw's violence. He watches his wife as she sleeps and is consumed with desire for her youth, her brown eyes and 'her hair, her hair!' so that we fear for her safety.

Good interpretation, identifies the theme

Very good. Shows the relationships between the poem's rhythm and theme

Very good. Compares the two poems

Highlights the final underlying mood

Overall comment: An in-depth answer, in which points are convincing and accompanied by supporting quotations embedded in sentences. There is also clear evidence of engagement with the poems and an imaginative interpretation of their meanings.

More could have been discussed on the disintegration of the relationship in 'Quickdraw' in verse three, but on the whole a very confident, well-written answer.

GRADE A

Further questions

EXAM-STYLE QUESTIONS

❶ What is the speaker of 'To His Coy Mistress' saying about love and why? Think about how he presents his argument.

❷ What are the similarities and differences between the betrayals in 'Sister Maude' and one other poem in *Relationships*?

❸ How is Time presented in 'Hour', and why? Choose another poem from the cluster in which time passes differently, and compare it with 'Hour'. Pay close attention to the imagery.

❹ In what ways are 'Sonnet 43' and 'Sonnet 116' similar? Think about:

- the theme of each poem

- the structure of each poem.

❺ Compare the ways poets present family relationships in 'Brothers' and one other poem in the cluster.

CONTROLLED ASSESSMENT-STYLE QUESTIONS

❶ Themes and ideas: explore the ways poets present and use ideas related to families in poems you have studied. Include comment on:

- what aspects of the family are conveyed through the language

- what kind of feelings are evoked in the reader.

❷ Themes and ideas: explore the ways in which poets use and present ideas about nature in the poems you have studied. In particular, comment on nature imagery and symbolism and its effect.

❸ Aspects of genre and form: explore the different ways poets have been inventive with their use of genre and form in the cluster, selecting a range of poems to comment on.

❹ Aspects of genre and form: compare the way poets use the sonnet form to explore ideas about love or desire with other poems with similar themes but with a different form and structure.

Literary terms

Literary term	Explanation
alliteration	where the same sound is repeated in a stretch of language, usually at the beginning of words
allusion	a reference in a work of literature to something outside the work, such as poetry, myth, or historical or biographical detail
ambiguity	when words or sentences have more than one meaning and it is not clear which is the true interpretation
assonance	when the same vowel sound appears in the same place in a series of words
ballad	a traditional form; a story written in rhyme with four lines to a verse
cadence	the repeating rise and fall of the rhythms of speech
caesura	a pause during a line of poetry
colloquial	the everyday speech used by people in ordinary situations
connotation	an additional meaning attached to a word in specific circumstances, i.e. what it suggests or implies
consonance	a repeated arrangements of consonants with a change in the vowel sound that separates them
couplet	two lines of poetry that are paired. See also rhyming couplet
dedicate	to address a poem, book or work to a person
denouement	the final part of a story, play or film
dialect	accent and vocabulary, varying by region and social background
dipodic	a light rocking metre of two feet (a unit of rhythm)
double rhyme	in which two final syllables rhyme, for example earful/tearful
enjambment	in poetry when a line runs on into the next, without pause, so carrying the thought with it. Sometimes called 'run-on line'
extended metaphor	in poetry a metaphor that continues some aspect of the image. It may continue into the next line, or throughout the poem. See also metaphor
figurative language	language that is not expressed plainly, but through imagery or figures of speech
free verse	verses without a regular rhythm, though they may contain some rhyme
ghazal	a traditional Eastern and Middle Eastern verse written in rhyming couplets about the beauty of love and the pain of separation
haiku	a Japanese nature poem of seventeen syllables, arranged 5,7,5, that captures a moment in time
hyperbole	the use of exaggeration for effect
iambic pentameter	a line of poetry consisting of five iambic feet (a foot being a unit of rhythm)
imagery	descriptive language that uses images to make actions, objects and characters more vivid in the reader's mind. Metaphors and similes are examples of imagery
imperative	expressing a command, as in: Come in!
irony	deliberately saying one thing when you mean another, usually in a humorous or sarcastic way
juxtaposition	contrasting ideas placed together
lament	a poem or song that expresses grief or mourning
metaphor	when one thing is used to describe another thing to create a striking or unusual image
metaphysical poets	the name given to a group of seventeenth-century poets who were concerned with analysis rather than feeling, and used complex and sometimes exaggerated imagery and clever, bold ideas.
motif	a repeated theme or idea
narrative poem	a poem that tells a story

Literary term	Explanation
paradox	a statement that seems to be a contradiction, but makes sense
personification	when things or ideas are treated as if they were people, with human attributes and feelings
Petrarchan sonnet (Italian sonnet)	a sonnet that has an *abba abba* rhyme scheme followed by a sestet *cdcdcd*, though the pattern may vary slightly
polysyllabic	words of more than one syllable
praise song	a poem written in celebration of a person, or the gods or animals
quatrain	four lines of verse. Can stand alone or be a repeating form in a poem
quintain	five lines of verse. Can stand alone or be a repeating form in a poem
refrain	repeated lines or groups of words that convey the same meaning
repetition	repeating words or patterns in a poem
rhyming couplet	two lines of poetry, usually the same length, that rhyme
run-on line	see **enjambment**
satire	a type of literature in which topical issues are ridiculed
sestet	a verse of six lines
sibilant	a hissing sound in speech made, for example, with an 's' or 'sh'
simile	when one thing is compared directly to another thing, using the words 'like' or 'as'
sonnet	a fourteen-line verse with a rhyming couplet at the end. The Shakespearean sonnet has an *abab cdcd efef gg* rhyme scheme
structure	the movement of a narrative or poem from beginning to end, or the form of a narrative or poem
theme	the idea (usually the main one) running through a work of literature
tone	the mood created by an artistic work
voice	the speaker or narrator of a poem or work of fiction that is created in the reader's mind

Checkpoint answers

Checkpoint 1
The 'flame tree's spread' evokes the mother's arms embracing the child or protecting the child from harm.

Checkpoint 2
The image conjures up a curled newborn baby. The image of a bud is especially appropriate because it has not yet developed into a flower, just as a baby is not yet a child or adult.

Checkpoint 3
'Like the shut of a winter's day', in the first verse, suggests how the farmer is 'shut' out of his wife's affections.

Checkpoint 4
This line could mean that the speaker's interest in the new love is more than a trip to Paris, or it could mean a fear that it will be.

Checkpoint 5
The plural 'we' suggests togetherness, which suits the lovers' intimacy.

Checkpoint 6
The image refers to 'Time', and 'Love' is not affected by it at all.

Checkpoint 7
'Nettles' uses images of war to refer to the pain caused by the nettles and also the pain the speaker' son will experience in life.

Checkpoint 8
It would be a suitable title because (a) the 'Last Chance saloon' suggests that the relationship is drawing to a close (b) the poem uses imagery from a typical Western.

Checkpoint 9
In verse three, 'hummed harmonics' is an example o alliteration using the letter 'h'. It recalls (along with the repetition of 'm') the resonant sound of the harmonium.

Checkpoint 10
The 'smile' suggests that the boys have an understanding that they will leave the younger chil behind, in order to 'stroll the town', doing what grown-ups do.